THE OFFICIAL
Wolves
ANNUAL 2019

Written by Paul Berry

Designed by Abbie Groom,
Synaxis Design Consultancy Ltd

g

A Grange Publication

© 2018. Published by Grange Communications Ltd., Edinburgh,
under licence from Wolverhampton Wanderers Football Club. Printed in the EU.

Photographs © AMA Sport Agency - Sam Bagnall, Dave Bagnall, Matt Ashton, James Baylis. SM2 Studio - Stuart Manley, Shaun Mallen, PA Images and the Wolves Archive.

ISBN: 978-1-912595-23-5

Contents

NUNO
had a dream

And so it transpired, that Nuno's dream, and that of thousands upon thousands of Wolves supporters, did actually come true!

A sensational first season in management in England, guiding Wolves to the Sky Bet Championship title in some style with some superb football, and 99 points into the bargain.

An instant hero in Wolverhampton, the Portuguese Head Coach did indeed build a football team to make a club, and a city, proud.

A charismatic presence, and one who was certainly itching to take on the Premier League challenge, here we take a look at some of Nuno's thoughts and quotes on a variety of issues!

Nuno on...
THE 2017/18 SEASON

"The project started last year when we embraced this challenge of coming to Wolves. We came and there was a bit of a challenge in front of us in one of the toughest competitions in the world.

"When you come and find something and you want to change you say 'Will this work with my idea, with my vision?'

"And the players - they believed in something that was changing.

"It was a special day when we all celebrated together. The parade on the bus was emotional and it was fantastic to see 30,000 people at the park."

Nuno on...
HIS BACKGROUND

"I spent two or three years in a process, of really trying to get inside football and look at my future. I learned a lot from the coaches I played for.

"And there are other things too. I played in Russia, in Spain, I was a part of the national team. You take everything you experience, and it is like you put it all in a box.

"Then, when you need anything from it, at any point, you go in and you grab it. It becomes an instinct."

"I don't really believe that there is something different in the Championship because football is the game. It's the same thing. It's the same. There are specific situations and characteristics of the Championship, but it's a competition. There are good teams, there are good players.

"Being a Wolf means a lot. It means you never give up, you support each other. The way we did it in the first year was absolutely amazing.

"The fans' support was incredible, for the players, singing the songs. I cannot thank the fans enough, but at the same time I am humble enough to ask: Let's do it again. Let's do it again. I know we are going to have the support, and we have to give back for that support. Together we are stronger."

"We wanted to create an identity with a shape and a formation that allowed us to go through the whole competition playing the same style and the same way.

"And then along the way to try and improve and find any solutions that were needed."

Nuno on...

HIS PLAYERS

"In my opinion, all my players could play in the top six.

"For me, my players are the best players in the world. And I say it again, the best players in the world. This is my belief and this is my conviction. It sounds absurd for some people maybe, but for me, no. It is my belief because it is the way I look at them. I admire them, I see them work, I don't make comparisons with nobody. They are the best, I hope they think they are."

Nuno on...

THE PREMIER LEAGUE

"We are now in step two, year two, and in the Premier League.

"Just look at the quality in the Premier League. The simple statistic of how many players of the Premier League were involved in the World Cup, that says a lot about the Premier League. No doubt about it and the best competition amongst clubs in the World.

"We are highly motivated for it and we are ready. We cannot control the expectations outside, that doesn't affect us.

"We did it before, over and over again last season, the same things many times, so why change? We won't change anything. Our routines are the same, and we just have to be better this season."

Nuno on...

HIS BACKROOM TEAM

"I am very thankful in the trust and the confidence that the club put in us as a technical team.

"We really work as a team. First of all we are friends, we respect each other, we admire each other and we work for the same goals. Each one of us has his own abilities and we look at each player to see

AUGUST
2017

Pre-season had brought the normal preparation and hard work ahead of the new campaign, but also the hugely sad news that popular keeper Carl Ikeme had been struck down by acute leukaemia.

Everyone rallied behind him, and a 24-hour penalty shootout in Wolfie's Den ahead of the opening day win against Middlesbrough was among a series of fundraising initiatives for Cure Leukaemia to show support and solidarity for the number one.

Excellent away wins at Derby and Hull made it three from three for Nuno's men before defeat at home to Cardiff and a draw at Brentford ever so slightly dented the early season optimism.

But there was certainly plenty to cheer about for the new look squad, signings including the likes of Willy Boly, Ruben Neves and Diogo Jota hitting the ground running despite their lack of Championship experience.

It was very much a sense of the changing of the guard at Molineux, and with several senior players having already departed in the close season, the popular pair of Dave Edwards and Nouha Dicko also bid farewell in August.

EFL Cup progress was secured scrappily at home to Yeovil but then in hugely impressive fashion at Southampton.

SEPTEMBER 2017

After seven games in August it was time for another seven in September, this time in a period of 22 days, as the ever-unforgiving Championship grind took hold.

But Wolves were relishing the task and relishing the challenge.

EFL Cup progress continued with a hard-fought solitary goal win against Bristol Rovers while the league brought four wins, two draws and one defeat, and that only after Conor Coady had been sent off in the early stages at Sheffield United.

Two of the wins came late, thanks to Diogo Jota against Nottingham Forest and Alfred N'Diaye against Barnsley, while Danny Batth also secured a point with a fine header against Bristol City late on.

Jota had started the month with a spectacular winner against Millwall and again finished it on the scoresheet as Wolves emphatically despatched Burton 4-0 to climb back into the automatic promotion spots, a position they were not to relinquish.

OCTOBER 2017

Wolves returned from the second international break of the season with the small matter of a Midlands derby against Aston Villa, on an electric Molineux night in front of over 30,000.

And Nuno's men duly delivered, putting on a tremendous display with goals from Diogo Jota and Leo Bonatini securing a convincing 2-0 win.

There was an equally fierce encounter at home to Preston seven days later, which Wolves edged 3-2, and, after a rare defeat at QPR, the month finished in positive fashion with a 2-0 victory against Norwich at Carrow Road.

And yet the highlight of the month was probably a game which Wolves lost, albeit only on penalties, as Will Norris and company defied Premier League champions elect Manchester City and Bright Enobakhare went so close at the other end in an EFL Cup tie which finished level and goalless after extra time.

NOVEMBER 2017

Any mention of Guy Fawkes had been enough in recent years to send Wolves fans into a cold sweat – in three successive Novembers the team had failed to win in 12 attempts.

Not this time though! Four games, four wins, and a continuing and growing feeling that Nuno and company were very much the real deal.

Barry Douglas, the King of Assists, set up Romain Saiss and Leo Bonatini in the 2-0 win against Fulham before the defence and John Ruddy did much to pave the way for victory by a similar scoreline at Reading.

Then Leeds and Bolton were convincingly despatched at Molineux, by 4-1 and 5-1 respectively, as that November curse was well and truly lifted.

DECEMBER
2017

December and the busy Christmas period, always a pivotal time, and coming just after Nuno had picked up the Manager of the Month award after a scintillating November.

Not so many goals scored during this month, but plenty of gritty defensive resistance, 1-0 away wins at Birmingham City and Sheffield Wednesday either side of a goalless draw at home against battling Sunderland.

Another 1-0 home win followed, against Mick McCarthy's Ipswich, and Wolves went 389 minutes without conceding a goal until Lee Gregory's opener in a lively 2-2 Boxing Day draw at Millwall.

Then came Bristol City. What a game to round off 2017. Danny Batth sent off, Nuno despatched to the stands, City going in front and then having their keeper sent off, Barry Douglas levelling and then setting up Ryan Bennett for an injury time headed winner.

Cue the celebrations.
Happy New Year one and all!

all-paye

JANUARY 2018

January brought shock and sadness off the pitch, with the sudden passings of long-time Wolves employee John 'Fozzie' Hendley and former Wolves striker and footballing pioneer Cyrille Regis.

Both were honoured prior to home fixtures, with Swansea and Nottingham Forest respectively.

On the pitch, there were mixed league results in the middle of the month with a draw at Barnsley and defeat at home to Forest but victories at the start and end of the month, at home to Brentford and away at Ipswich, secured Wolves a 12-point cushion at the top of the table.

That win at Portman Road came after a warm weather training camp in Marbella which certainly seemed to have the desired result in returning Wolves to winning ways.

In the FA Cup the 0-0 draw at home to Swansea provided Will Norris with a fifth clean sheet of the season but he was to concede a first goal in 491 minutes when the Welsh side prevailed 2-1 in the replay.

FEBRUARY 2018

Wolves played three home matches during the month of February, and powered into a 2-0 lead in all of them.

The first was the best, excellent goals in different ways from Ruben Neves and Diogo Jota and then a third from Ivan Cavaleiro securing a comfortably impressive 3-0 win against Sheffield United.

The other two games proved more nervy, holding on to a 2-1 lead against QPR and then seeing the advantage disappear thanks to a last gasp Norwich equaliser in a 2-2 draw.

Fortunes away from home were not to prove so fruitful, albeit in tough assignments against two teams very much involved in the promotion shake-up.

A 1-1 draw at Preston in the middle of the month was followed at the end by a 2-0 defeat at an all-conquering Fulham side who stretched their unbeaten run to 12.

MARCH

2018

Season Review
2017/18

Two big away trips for the start of March, and two very contrasting results.

First up a clinical 3-0 demolition of Leeds United at Elland Road, before Aston Villa's second half performance saw an initially tight contest end in a 4-1 win for the hosts as Wolves suffered a second defeat in three.

But teams with promotion aspirations always hit back after a defeat, and that is exactly what transpired as Nuno's men picked up six points in five days thanks to home victories against Reading and Burton.

Nothing however could prepare for a dramatic trip to Middlesbrough on Good Friday.

Wolves led 2-0, were reduced to nine men following the dismissals of Ruben Neves and Matt Doherty, conceded in added time, but somehow held on for the win to spark wild celebrations as Nuno charged onto the pitch at the full time whistle.

APRIL 2018

April was one of the more dramatic Aprils in Wolves' recent history.

A goal on league debut for substitute and Academy scholar Oskar Buur Rasmussen to secure a point at home to Hull was a decent enough story.

But that had nothing on two missed Cardiff penalties in added time as Wolves won 1-0 in Wales thanks to another Ruben Neves thunderbolt.

Neves still had more to come, an even better goal against Derby, after which Fulham's failure to beat Brentford secured Wolves' promotion the night before a 2-0 win against Birmingham.

The title then followed seven days later with a stunning 4-0 win at Bolton, and a 0-0 draw for the final home game of the season against Sheffield Wednesday could not dampen the celebrations as the Sky Bet Championship trophy was handed over.

MAY
2018

Just the one game in May, and not one of massive significance as things turned out.

They would have been disappointed to have finished the season with a 3-0 defeat at already relegated Sunderland, which saw Wolves finish on a tantalising 99 points, but the hard work had long been done. Promotion secured, the Sky Bet Championship secured, and now it was celebration time.

An open-top bus parade through the City Centre following a civic reception, and then on-stage appearances at West Park and Starworks Warehouse made for a truly fantastic Bank Holiday Monday before the annual End of Season dinner attracted record numbers on the Tuesday night.

It was a special night, started by Robert Plant, and highlighted by the ability of Ruben Neves, who claimed both the Supporters' and Players' Player of the Year awards, and Goal of the Season for his stupendous strike against Derby.

GOOD TIMES!

Celebrate good times, come on!

Wolves certainly did that, and well deserved it was too, after such a fantastic season.

Just as with the previous promotion to the Premier League back in 2009, there were three post-match chances to savour the success this time around.

The home game with Birmingham to toast promotion, the trip to Bolton where victory secured the title, and then back to Molineux against Sheffield Wednesday to lift the trophy.

And all this having enjoyed Brentford's draw at Fulham at the Novotel Hotel the night before the Blues fixture which had actually secured promotion. Here is a pictorial look back courtesy of Sam Bagnall and Dave Bagnall.

OUT OF DARKNESS
COMETH LIGHT!

The Wolverhampton city motto could have been coined for May 7th, 2018.

Yes there have been plenty of good times during the recent Wolverhampton Wanderers rollercoaster ride but, for the first time in 15 years, the city came to a standstill for an open top bus parade to savour Wolves' magnificent success. And the sun shone, so yes indeed, the city was bathed in light and gold! The bus, emblazoned with Ikeme 1 on the front, edged its way through the City Centre before the players took to the stage for party time at West Park, and then again at the Starworks Warehouse afterwards.

**Here are a few photos from a memorable day –
and we may have had just a little bit of fun with the captions....**

I don't think you're going to find them, Morgan.

Yeh I'm just out and about in town, having fun with a few friends...

Ruben's Mr Tickle impression is always a winner.

Slower than the Grand National this.

Who fancies a game of 'catch'?

It's no good folks – I can't change it to red.

Watch the trees, lads!

No Morgan, definitely not going to find them.

'Ey Benik, did you pay before you got on?'

Nice luxurious penthouse with a stately feel & a lovely balcony view. Bit busy outside though.

Danny, I've shrunk the Mikey....

Yes Morgan, there they are!

Kortney suddenly wondering if he has left his oven on.

No not me... take this lot instead.

Having a gander – from the Goose.

Where's Shakespeare? I'm ready for my balcony scene.

Sorry lads, changed timetable today.

Wonder if this flies like a javelin?

When the paparazzi get papped.

Worst karaoke double act ever.

Are you sure they are coming this way?

RUBEN'S SIX OF THE BEST

★★★★★★★

Of the many, many things which Ruben Neves did exceptionally well during his first season in English football with Wolves, scoring spectacular goals was right up there. In fact the Portuguese Prince, the Midfield Maestro, only did the spectacular. All of his six goals came from outside the penalty area, and all were superb. Little wonder that Neves claimed a hat trick of awards at the End of Season dinner, Goal of the Season along with the Supporters' and Players' Player of the Year accolades.

Let's take a look back....

 #1
15th August 2017
A Howitzer against Hull

 #2
15th December 2017
Man Friday against Wednesday

 #3
2th January 2018
A belter against Brentford

 #4
3rd February 2018
A swerver against Sheffield

 #5
6th April 2018
A corker against Cardiff

 #6
11th April 2018
Ruben versus the Rams

What a first season for Ruben Neves. He could have had his very own Goal of the Season competition. Unsurprisingly the memorable strike against Derby County sealed the Wolves award, described by many as the best goal seen at Molineux in many a year. Which was enjoyed just as much by his team-mates, as this picture shows. **Way to go Ruben!**

A star is born! Neves collects a pass from Barry Douglas over towards the left, takes a touch inside, and then lets fly. Hull keeper Allan McGregor has been a regular Scotland international, but he had absolutely no chance!

The Sky Sports cameras witnessed this one as Ivan Cavaleiro's free kick was only partially cleared. From just outside the 'D', Neves strolled up and expertly guided a low shot into the bottom corner of the net. Practically perfect precision in every way!

The first of two successful free kicks Neves despatched during the season. Leo Bonatini is fouled just outside the box, near the inside left channel. Our man steps up, and deliciously sends the ball over the wall and into the top corner to break the deadlock.

Another 3-0 home win, and another Neves masterclass to get things going. The ball breaks after Ivan Cavaleiro is tackled and Neves knows exactly what he is going to do. One touch out of his feet, and then the most sumptuous of strikes with his instep to curl the ball from outside the target and bring it back inside the far post. Sweet as.

Cometh the hour, cometh the Neves! Arguably the biggest game of the season, first traveling to second with the title still very much up for grabs. Having already had one sighter, the bearded Wanderer pops home another magnificent free kick from some distance, eventually, somehow, proving the only goal of the game to clinch a vital three points.

Saving the best till last. The cream of the crop. A corner is cleared, and Neves's first touch isn't the best as he flicks the ball up, ever so slightly behind him. But that makes the second touch even better, a dipping volley which arrows its way into the top corner past another international keeper in Scott Carson. Unbelievable stuff.

SNAP SHOT
of a season

SM2 Studio photographers have captured the rollercoaster ride for Wolves supporters for many years now.

Well last year must rank as one of the best, given the success of the team in storming to the Sky Bet Championship title!

Even then, there are always contrasting emotions watching a game of football, and here we take a snapshot of some of SM2's snaps of the Molineux faithful.

WOLFIE'S FUN PAGE

Howlers...

Why don't grasshoppers watch football?

Because they watch cricket instead.

← COLOUR ME IN!

Spot the Difference

Can you find the 6 differences between these two pictures?

Did you know?
Football players run six miles per game on average.

Answers on page 61

Getting Cross

Can you follow the lines to see which cross makes it into the goal?

Printing Problems!

Can you unjumble the names to reveal who these shirts belong to?

TOJA

IOBTAINN

Howlers...

Why was the chicken kicked off the football team?

For persistent fowl play.

They egged me on!

Player mix-up!

Photos of six of the Wolves squad have been mixed up! Can you tell who they are using the clues?

1
2
3

4
5
6

1. I'm Wolves number 16 and originally come from Liverpool.

2. I represented Portugal at the 2014 Toulon football Tournament – and no – I don't like coffee!

3. I've been at Wolves since August 2016, when I moved from Monaco.

4. I'm 6 feet and four inches tall, which really helps in my position!

5. I play as a central defender for Wolves, and wear the number 15 shirt.

6. I'm Wolves number 8, and I was voted Wolves player of the season in 2018.

THE BIG Wolves WORDSEARCH

It's here! The big Wolves Annual wordsearch is back, and this time we're focusing on the goalscorers. Or rather every single Wolves player who scored a goal, in any competition, during the 2017/18 Championship winning season.

There are a total of 19 to find, and we have included their full names – and, just for fun, we have added in the gaffer as well to bring it up to a round 20. We hope you enjoy the goal hunt as much as they did!

- ALFRED N'DIAYE
- BARRY DOUGLAS
- BENIK AFOBE
- BRIGHT ENOBAKHARE
- CONOR COADY
- DANNY BATTH
- DIOGO JOTA
- DONOVAN WILSON
- HELDER COSTA
- IVAN CAVALEIRO
- LEO BONATINI
- MATT DOHERTY
- NOUHA DICKO
- NUNO ESPIRITO SANTO
- OSKAR BUUR RASMUSSEN
- ROMAIN SAISS
- RYAN BENNETT
- RUBEN NEVES
- RUBEN VINAGRE
- WILLY BOLY

Answers on page 61.

L	W	O	I	Y	T	U	W	O	R	U	B	E	N	V	I	N	A	G	R	E	H	J	C	O
C	B	N	B	G	Z	A	L	E	O	C	T	T	E	N	N	E	B	N	A	Y	R	M	Q	T
O	L	V	A	H	A	N	B	X	K	G	S	Y	H	F	U	T	F	T	B	S	N	G	D	N
Y	J	V	Y	S	W	B	A	I	P	M	L	U	S	M	Y	R	K	R	E	L	Z	O	I	A
Q	Q	Y	T	F	I	B	R	I	G	H	T	E	N	O	B	A	K	H	A	R	E	W	O	S
C	U	D	R	T	X	R	R	W	C	I	R	V	O	A	U	Z	X	L	N	T	C	P	G	O
O	O	K	E	U	O	Z	Y	J	X	N	G	C	W	B	V	T	I	L	O	E	W	S	O	T
U	S	N	H	D	F	C	D	M	O	I	M	U	K	D	O	S	G	E	U	I	R	N	J	I
X	M	E	O	N	L	T	O	Y	S	R	Y	A	Q	U	D	N	W	R	H	D	A	X	O	R
G	I	S	D	R	B	F	U	H	W	N	F	X	T	L	O	L	A	E	A	Y	X	E	T	I
Y	J	S	T	Y	C	O	G	W	L	T	Y	I	P	S	B	K	U	T	D	P	J	Y	A	P
V	U	U	T	P	E	O	L	S	R	U	S	H	L	E	N	J	M	V	I	Y	A	C	E	S
O	I	M	A	R	L	J	A	Z	H	E	W	I	T	Z	B	H	N	P	C	N	X	F	J	E
Z	V	S	M	B	G	K	S	D	V	G	W	S	X	Q	T	O	S	O	K	A	I	V	S	O
B	A	A	S	H	U	Y	Q	E	Y	N	A	A	H	U	W	H	F	R	O	U	M	N	F	N
M	N	R	B	C	T	P	N	P	A	L	F	R	E	D	N	D	I	A	Y	E	J	E	P	U
T	C	R	S	N	T	N	F	V	Y	O	D	K	L	V	X	M	V	B	K	N	H	Z	K	N
Y	A	U	E	A	E	Y	O	N	L	K	B	A	D	K	J	A	H	Q	E	I	L	W	O	Z
I	V	U	R	B	J	N	O	I	O	D	R	Y	E	O	F	L	Y	D	O	K	N	V	A	R
S	A	B	U	X	O	N	D	M	B	X	Q	Z	R	C	S	P	W	U	I	T	J	E	I	P
Q	L	R	H	D	P	M	R	C	Y	R	V	S	C	F	K	G	K	I	H	G	T	H	B	Y
L	E	A	U	O	G	E	R	W	L	X	H	R	O	M	A	I	N	S	A	I	S	S	Z	S
O	I	K	S	P	B	U	Y	C	L	G	U	T	S	Y	E	F	D	L	G	Y	U	M	L	W
H	R	S	K	E	A	F	H	S	I	A	T	G	T	Q	H	T	T	A	B	Y	N	N	A	D
T	O	O	X	Y	S	I	T	L	W	P	S	R	A	O	M	N	R	J	R	C	B	Q	W	O

27

RAUL JIMENEZ

"I wanted a **NEW CHALLENGE** and I want to do my best to HELP THE TEAM BE NEAR THE TOP.

I have a lot of achievements from before, but **I WANT MORE.**"

Raul Jimenez, part of Mexico's squad at the 2018 World Cup, arrived at Wolves on a season long loan from Benfica. Jimenez secured multiple team honours with Benfica, having moved there from Atletico Madrid.

NEW faces:

JONNY CASTRO OTTO

Jonny Castro Otto, a full back by trade who can play on either side, joined Wolves on a season-long loan from Atletico Madrid, whom he had just joined from Celta Vigo. Jonny spent six years in total with Celta, and is an under-21 international with Spain.

Wolves' exciting project *has given me* **THE OPPORTUNITY** TO PLAY HERE AND IN THE PREMIER LEAGUE, *which is the* **best in the world.**

NEW faces:

RUI PATRICIO

The signing of Portuguese international goalkeeper Rui Patricio, who was in the nets when his country won the 2016 European. Championships, was a huge statement of intent from Wolves. Patricio joined from Sporting Lisbon, whom he had been with since the age of 12, a total of 18 years.

"It's one of my objectives to play in the **PREMIER LEAGUE** and now is the opportunity, and I **WANT TO HELP THE TEAM** and the players in the club **TO PROGRESS.**"

NEW faces:

JOÃO MOUTINHO

Midfield maestro Moutinho arrived at Molineux as Portugal's third most capped player, with 113 international appearances to his name, including the 2018 World Cup. He started his career with Sporting Lisbon and went on to win league titles with Porto and Monaco respectively.

ADAMA TRAORE

"People who know me know I like **TO WORK HARD, TO PUSH MYSELF EVERY DAY.** My mentality is to work every day **AND BE PREPARED** for whatever comes."

Adama Traore, who defines the description 'jet-heeled winger', was the latest to become Wolves' record signing when arriving from Middlesbrough shortly before the start of the 2018/19 season. The pacey Spaniard, who started his career by turning out for Barcelona's 'B' team, first moved to the Midlands by joining Aston Villa before spending two seasons by the Riverside with 'Boro.

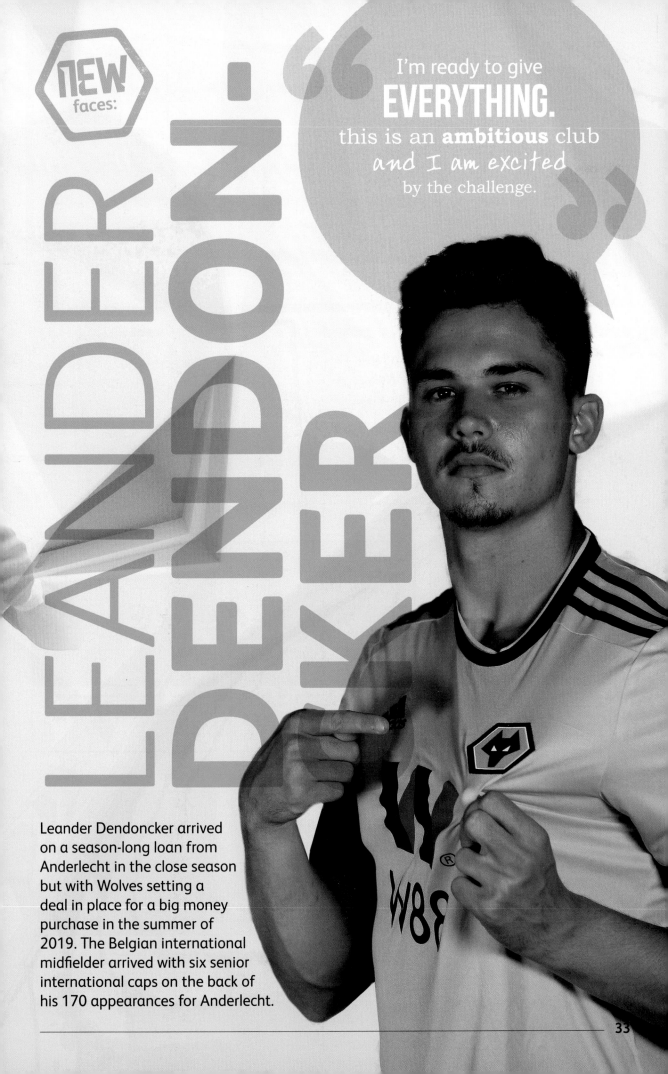

LEANDER DENDON-
LEANDER DENDONKER

"I'm ready to give **EVERYTHING.** this is an **ambitious** club and I am excited by the challenge."

Leander Dendoncker arrived on a season-long loan from Anderlecht in the close season but with Wolves setting a deal in place for a big money purchase in the summer of 2019. The Belgian international midfielder arrived with six senior international caps on the back of his 170 appearances for Anderlecht.

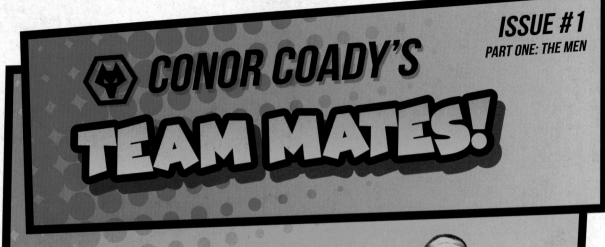

CONOR COADY'S
TEAM MATES!

Time then to take a closer look at the personalities that make up the Wolves Men and the Wolves Women squads.

Conor Coady, who skippered the team on many occasions during the 2017/18 season, lifts the lid on his team-mates in the Molineux dressing room.

BEST TRAINER

Tough question that.
Everyone trains well, obviously! If I have to pick I would say Ruben Neves. He works really hard during the session and then stays out afterwards to do other bits and bobs as well.

WORST TRAINER

Doc. Matt Doherty. By a million miles. He is just horrific. Looks like a bag of rags when he arrives and it all goes on from there.

WORST FASHION

Doc. Again. All day long. His tracksuits, his stupid socks. I don't know if he thinks it is his trademark but it is all a bit daft to be honest.

BEST MUSICAL TASTES

The changing room DJ is Helder Costa. And he does ok to be fair. Music is music to me, I am not really that bothered, but Helder looks after if for us and does a good job.

WORST MUSICAL TASTES

As I said I'm not too hot on music either way. But there was one time in pre-season when Bonatini had some Brazilian music on in the dressing room. And I didn't really get it. So I will say him.

BEST FASHION

Best clobber? What do we think. It would have been Barry Douglas but he has gone now. Who has a go? Do you know what? We have had one or two nights out and Cav (Ivan Cavaleiro) has a good go on a night out. His gear is a bit out there as well. So I'd say Ivan.

WORST BANTER

Will Norris. He comes out with some lines and I don't really understand them. He thinks he is really funny, and I don't think he is. So I will give that one to Nozza

BEST BANTER

I have hammered him a bit but I have to say I do find Doc really funny. He's got a good craic. He has got all the one-liners and he does make me laugh, I'll give him that!

MOST SKILFUL

We've got a few now haven't we? I'd have to say Costa. He is really tough to play against in training. He can turn you both ways and has got that balance on both feet. And is so quick with it.

TOUGHEST TACKLER

Danny Batth. Without a doubt. He just clobbers everyone. It doesn't matter what exercise or drill he is doing in training – Danny will clobber you.

NOT-SO-TOUGH TACKLER

Tricky one this. I don't think anyone has an issue about putting their foot in when they need to! I'd maybe go with Diogo Jota and that is only sometimes in training just because he keeps himself out of trouble. But in a game he doesn't pull out of anything.

LEAST SKILFUL

I think I am going to be have to put my hand up for this one. I'll be up there for that one. I don't mind admitting I'm not the most skilful.

MOST INTELLIGENT

Will Norris. Very intelligent fella. He has got his head screwed on and is very intelligent.

MOST DOPEY

Oh no! We're back to Doc again. He's just a bag of rags isn't he? And he knows it as well. I do love him really though.

HAPPIEST

Well it certainly isn't Benno (Ryan Bennett). He is one of the most miserable men I have ever met. Saiss is quite happy though. He often has a smile on his face and is bobbing about a bit.

BEST YOU'VE PLAYED AGAINST

I'd go back to the FA Cup tie against Chelsea a couple of seasons ago and I'd say Eden Hazard. What a top player he is.

BEST YOU'VE PLAYED WITH

Another tough one this as I am fortunate to have played with some great players, especially here at Wolves. I'd have to say Ruben Neves. He is absolutely class isn't he? On a different level.

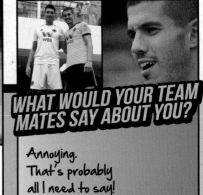

WHAT WOULD YOUR TEAM MATES SAY ABOUT YOU?

Annoying. That's probably all I need to say!

ANNA PRICE'S TEAM MATES!

We have heard from Conor Coady about the men's team, now it's time to lift the lid on the Wolves Women dressing room and find out more about the players and personalities which makes up the ladies' squad.

For this we turned to captain Anna Price, to tell us more in part two of our Team Mates feature!

BEST TRAINER

Andrea Whetton. She won the Player of the Season award last season. She is a quiet girl, but just gets on with it and trains really hard. She is always at training, always on time, and works her socks off.

WORST TRAINER

Jenny Anslow. Sorry Jen! She is an unbelievable player. But as for training? She rocks up 30 minutes late with a Costa or a Starbucks in hand. Then she'll go and have a rubdown. And then join in and show all of us just how good she is!

WORST FASHION

Worst?
What do you mean?
There is no worst!
We are a squad of very fashionable ladies!

BEST MUSICAL TASTES

I'd say Crids for this one, Charlotte Criddle. She has started to take over the playlist in the dressing room since she signed, and likes the same sort of upbeat tunes as me to get the dressing room going. And she's not so much of a fan of music with 'no words'! So that will do for me.

WORST MUSICAL TASTES

I am one of the older players in the squad, and so end up having to listen to a lot of R&B, House and Dance music that is 'in' at the present time. Tough one but Natalie Widdal I would say has the worst. There is some good in there, but definitely some bad in there as well! Music with no words, which, as I have already mentioned, some of us don't really like!

BEST FASHION

Natalie Widdal again! She is very fashionable and always up to date. She does a lot of shopping (I don't know how much now being a homeowner) but Natalie certainly takes a lot of pride in her appearance, and deserves this one!

WORST BANTER

I can't say anyone for that. It's not like girls to be nasty is it? We are all really nice to each other and get on so there is no one that stands out for their banter not being up to standards.

BEST BANTER

Claire Hakeman. Comfortably.
Claire played for Wolves for a long time after being at Birmingham before that so she has been involved in a lot of different dressing rooms. She is really quick-witted and loves the banter. It is a shame she has now retired after a great career. We are going to need someone else to step up!

MOST SKILFUL

Chloe Williams is an absolute baller, she came into the first team last season at 16 and is teaching us a thing or two for sure! Massive talent and one for the future in the women's game.

TOUGHEST TACKLER

Tammi George. She came into the team at the age of 16 but is not scared of anything. She never shies away from a challenge and will throw herself into a challenge with any age or size of opponent despite being so young.

NOT-SO-TOUGH TACKLER

This is a tough one, excuse the pun. No one is ever avoiding a tough tackle. Maybe I'll go for Emma Cross. Only because although she plays at centre half, she reads the game so well and is so skilful that she doesn't really need to put herself about too much. And she is a really nice person as well!

LEAST SKILFUL

Tough one but going to say Mai Butler. She is an out-and-out centre half – strong, solid and a ball winner, we don't want her doing any tricks on the edge of our box to be honest. Leave that to the attackers!

MOST INTELLIGENT

The twins! Emma and Jade Cross. They are both really clever, and also fairly quiet. But they train really hard and have high standards. An asset to the team.

MOST DOPEY

I have gone for Billie Haynes for this one, she comes out with some absolute classics! Not the sharpest but wouldn't have her any other way.

HAPPIEST

Mai Butler for this one as well. She is always happy, always positive and always encouraging. No matter how training is going, or how a match is going, she is always upbeat.

BEST YOU'VE PLAYED AGAINST

I played against a lot of the top players back in the day. Karen Carney, Fara Williams and Eni Aluko. For the best I'd probably say Kelly Smith.

BEST YOU'VE PLAYED WITH

I have been fortunate to play with a lot of really good players. If I had to narrow it down, I'd probably say Sally Stanton and Emily Westwood, who both eventually moved on to play for Birmingham in the Super League.

WHAT WOULD YOUR TEAM MATES SAY ABOUT YOU?

That I am positive and encouraging as a captain. Hopefully anyway! And that I've always got my sun cream with me – as a fair-skinned ginger!

Thanks to Simon Faulkner Photography for all the photos. Simon is Wolves Women's regular matchday photographer. Check out facebook.com/simonfphoto for more of his photos. He can be contacted via email at simon.faulkner1@gmail.com.

f /simonfphoto ✉ simon.faulkner1@gmail.com

WORLD CUP WOLVES

There were three players on show at the 2018 World Cup who then reported back, albeit a little bit later, to Wolves for pre-season.

Defender Romain Saiss, with Morocco, and summer signings Rui Patricio (Portugal) and loanee Raul Jimenez (Mexico).

There were also plenty of Wolves fans out in Russia, as well as a couple of former members of the backroom staff.

And who could forget that we have our very own World Cup winner in the ranks, Morgan Gibbs-White, a winner with England Under-17s in India towards the back end of 2017.

As shown by these photos a fair few Wolves fans made the trip to Russia to support England. And there is also some former Wolves influence within the England backroom staff.

Former Wolves Head of Medical Steve Kemp is pictured with Jordan Henderson, whilst former Wolves masseur Ben Mortlock is another who is part of the team behind the scenes.

MORGAN GIBBS-WHITE

It certainly hasn't been a bad rise to prominence for Wolves Academy graduate Morgan Gibbs-White. The attacking midfielder made his first team bow for Wolves at a young age, and then went on to be one of England's key performers as they won the Under-17 World Cup. Back at Molineux, he was presented with a special framed shirt as a memento by full England international and Wolves Vice-President Steve Bull, and Academy Manager Gareth Prosser.

RAUL JIMENEZ

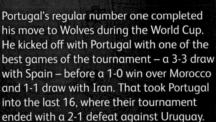

Season-long loan signing Raul Jimenez came off the bench in Mexico's first and last games of the tournament, the 1-0 win against Germany and the 2-0 defeat to Brazil in the last 16. In the other two group games – a 2-1 win against South Korea and 3-0 defeat against Sweden – the striker was an unused substitute.

RUI PATRICIO

Portugal's regular number one completed his move to Wolves during the World Cup. He kicked off with Portugal with one of the best games of the tournament – a 3-3 draw with Spain – before a 1-0 win over Morocco and 1-1 draw with Iran. That took Portugal into the last 16, where their tournament ended with a 2-1 defeat against Uruguay.

ROMAIN SAISS

Romain Saiss's World Cup finished with Morocco with an impressive 2-2 draw against Spain which included an equally impressive goal-line clearance. But 1-0 defeats against Iran and Portugal, of which Saiss played 90 minutes of the former, meant that they were already out of the competition prior to that game.

GOOD LUCK, CARL!

For all the great celebrations and wonderful memories created during the 2017/18 Wolves season, arguably the best piece of news came when a tweet from Carl Ikeme landed in the early afternoon of Saturday, June 23rd. 'After a year of intense chemotherapy, I would like to share that I am in complete REMISSION,' began Carl, signalling the end to a hugely difficult and gruelling year following his diagnosis with leukaemia. There is of course more treatment to come, and more hurdles to battle, but that was just the news everyone wanted to hear from Wolves' popular former keeper. That Carl then announced his retirement just over a month later was perhaps not a complete surprise, choosing to focus on his health and indeed future opportunities, hopefully some of which would still involve football.

The groundswell of support from past and present team-mates, Wolves staff and supporters was matched by the city of Wolverhampton and wider football community as a whole. And, in reflecting on a fantastic career totalling 274 appearances between the sticks, of which 207 came for Wolves, it was time for Carl to consider a new chapter in his life. All Wolves supporters will wish him the very best for that future – good luck Carl!

B

FOUNDATION
DB CONTINUING TO DEVELOP

It has been another busy year for Wolves club captain Danny Batth and his partner Natalie in the development of their charity – Foundation DB.

In last year's Annual we carried photos of their visit to India and the YUWA Academy, one of the charities they support.

This year the documentary filmed and produced by Natalie including that visit – Married to the Game – premiered in London and Wolverhampton with proceeds from the nights and subsequent streaming going to the charity in India.

Last Christmas Danny and Natalie also supported one of their other charities – YMCA Open Door in the Black Country – by visiting some of the young people living with host families.Danny has also raised further funds by auctioning items of Wolves memorabilia donated by himself and team-mates, and encouraging people to take part in running events.

Here are a few photos from a busy year for Foundation DB.

FOUNDATION B
🐦 @Foundation__DB

Photograph by
Nik Andrews Photography

VONOVIA RUHRSTADION

A short walk for the team from hotel to stadium in Germany.

Rafa Mir celebrates scoring against Basel.

Ruben reports for duty!

Wolves into
EUROPE!

Wolves embarked on a mini European tour as part of their pre-season preparations ahead of the 2018/19 campaign.

First of all there was a week spent in the picturesque town of Vevey on the shores of Lake Geneva in Switzerland, and wins against FC Basel (2-1) and Young Boys (4-0) which saw them return home with the Uhrencup.

It was a more fleeting trip to Bochum in Germany to get more minutes under the belt in the H-Hotels Cup, with goalless draws over 45 minutes against VFL Bochum 1848 (Wolves losing 5-4 on penalties) and Real Betis Balompie seeing the team finish in joint third.

Here are a selection of photos from the trips from Sam Bagnall and James Baylis.

Ryan Giles was one of a number of young players on the trip.

Heads you win! Ryan Bennett on the ball!

They shoot, he saves! Rui Patricio with two penalty stops on debut.

Watching the penalties against Bochum.

Leo Bonatini on target in the Alps.

Some instructions from Nuno for Morgan Gibbs-White.

Raul Jimenez in his first Wolves action in the H-Hotels Cup.

It's Coming Home! Danny Batth and Conor Coady with the Uhrencup.

Nuno looking on.

Picturesque surroundings in Switzerland.

A happy Helder!

Warm-ups in the hills.

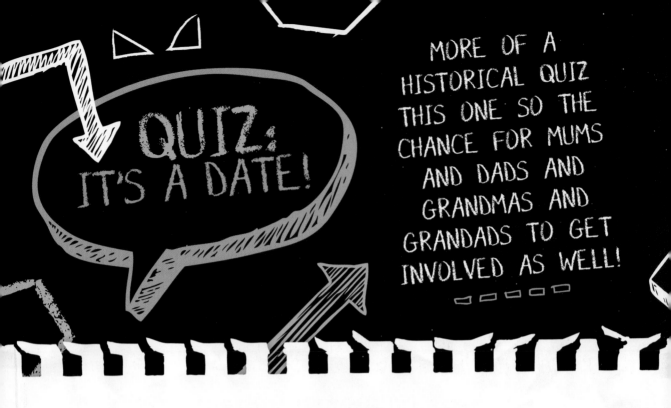

QUIZ: IT'S A DATE!

MORE OF A HISTORICAL QUIZ THIS ONE SO THE CHANCE FOR MUMS AND DADS AND GRANDMAS AND GRANDADS TO GET INVOLVED AS WELL!

 1 Sir Jack Hayward, later to become Wolves' Chairman and President, was born in Dunstall.

 (A) JANUARY   **(B) JUNE**   **(C) MARCH**

 2 Steve Bull scored the first of his 306 goals for Wolves, away at Cardiff, in the Freight Rover Trophy.

 (A) OCTOBER   **(B) NOVEMBER**   **(C) DECEMBER**

 3 Derek Parkin made the last of his 609 appearances for Wolves, still a club record. Wolves lost 3-1 to Aston Villa.

 (A) MARCH   **(B) APRIL**   **(C) MAY**

 4 A midfielder by the name of Kenny Hibbitt made his debut for Wolves following his earlier move from Bradford Park Avenue.

 (A) AUGUST   **(B) JANUARY**   **(C) APRIL**

 5 1972, and Wolves' only appearance in a European final to date, a tense two-legged affair with Tottenham Hotspur.

 (A) MARCH   **(B) APRIL**   **(C) MAY**

 6 Back in 1989, Wolves and West Bromwich Albion met for the first time in the second tier in 58 years. Robbie Dennison's goal and a Mark Kendall penalty save paved the way for a last gasp Bully winner and a 2-1 victory.

 (A) SEPTEMBER   **(B) OCTOBER**   **(C) NOVEMBER**

We have taken one event from each month of the year in Wolves' history. All you need to do is pair up the right event, to the right month.

Each month of the year is the answer to only one question, and, just to help out, we have given you some options.

Good luck!

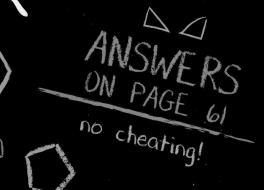
ANSWERS ON PAGE 61

no cheating!

 7 Goals from Richard Stearman and Andreas Weimann helped Wolves to an impressive 2-1 FA Cup win against Liverpool at Anfield.

 (A) JANUARY   (B) FEBRUARY   (C) MARCH

 8 "MM stands for Mick McCarthy, not Merlin the Magician." Quite an opening press conference from Wolves new boss!

 (A) JUNE   (B) JULY   (C) AUGUST

 9 The end of an era with the departure of Dave Jones, the first manager to take Wolves into the Premier League.

 (A) OCTOBER   (B) NOVEMBER   (C) DECEMBER

 10 John Richards became the first, and still only, Wolves player to come off the bench in a game and score a hat trick, in an FA Cup tie against Charlton in 1976.

 (A) FEBRUARY   (B) MARCH   (C) APRIL

11 The still popular Peter Knowles made his final Wolves appearance at the age of 23, a 3-3 home draw with Nottingham Forest in 1969.

 (A) MAY   (B) SEPTEMBER   (C) OCTOBER

12 Billy Wright made his Wolves debut, and it wasn't a bad one at that, a 6-1 home victory against Arsenal.

 (A) AUGUST   (B) SEPTEMBER   (C) OCTOBER

Karthi
OF THE WOLVES!

Karthi Gnanasegaram is an accomplished broadcaster who can be seen on many different TV and radio programmes, particularly in the worlds of sport and music. Karthi is also a keen Wolves fan, who keeps

up with the team's fortunes wherever her work may take her! We are delighted that she agreed to talk to the Wolves Annual.

Hi Karthi, thanks for talking to us! A Wolves fan, reading out the sports news on the BBC, amongst many other things! First things first, how did you become a Wolves fan?

I'm not from a football family so I got into football through school really. Although I lived in Wolverhampton throughout my entire school life, we went to King Edward's in Birmingham so had a long daily commute. The Girls' School was on the same land as King Edward's Boys' School so everything apart from lessons was mixed and there was a bond between those of us from Wolverhampton that had to do the hour-and-a-half commute each way to school and back. I think that cemented my Wolves identity, despite being at school in Birmingham with West Brom and Villa fans. I spent most of my non-school life at Linden Lea Tennis Club which has moved recently and is now next to the Wolves Academy so would be a great tennis club for me to rejoin...if I lived there! By the way, I cannot wait to read out Wolves results on the BBC1 news at the weekends!

What are your early memories of supporting Wolves?

My earliest memories of Wolves are of Steve Bull. I remember the papers always having pictures of Bully on the front and back pages, and Wolves winning the Fourth and

Third Divisions so I'd missed the turmoil of previous years! We did a school project about the number of female fans at football games around the country and I still have the letter that Wolves sent back to us!

Do you have any particular Wolves heroes or special games that stand out?

Bully - obviously! I even tried to go to his restaurant with Jacqui Oatley when we were both back in Wolverhampton for Christmas one year but couldn't quite co-ordinate our diaries! My favourite memory has got to be the 2003 play-off final at the Millennium Stadium. I hadn't been there before so the whole trip was such a ridiculously exciting day out. I remember still being nervous when we were 3-0 up by half time but eventually calmed down and to make it even more amusing, a Sheffield United friend was there with us! I had never seen Wolves playing in the Premier League but it was finally going to happen.

Let's talk about your career. When did you decide you wanted to become involved in journalism and broadcasting?

I come from a family of doctors so didn't know about any other professions when I was growing up. Mum and Dad played badminton with someone who presented the sports bulletins on the local radio station in Wolverhampton and I would get very excited whenever Tony was on the radio, so one day they arranged for me to go and visit him at work. I thought it was the most amazing, exciting job, having never previously realised that you could make something like that a career, and decided immediately that was what I wanted to do and never wavered. When I had to do work experience after my GCSEs, I applied to the Wolverhampton Express and Star and as it was during Wimbledon they asked me to write a few articles which they ended up publishing! I was so excited to see my writing in the paper and still have them somewhere. As I wanted to go to Cambridge University and they don't do any media courses, I had to make sure I kept doing something in broadcasting while I was studying so worked at the local radio station, which was very much against the university's rules! You weren't allowed to have a job as you were supposed to put all your efforts in to studying!

You have been involved in so many different programmes and broadcast mediums... what are you involved with currently?

Quite a lot at the moment! Doing Wimbledon for BBC Radio 5 Live is always a highlight of my year and even though it meant missing my first World Cup since 2006, I absolutely love working for the Wimbledon team. This year I covered my first US Open tennis tournament for work, as opposed to my previous trips to Flushing Meadows as a sports fan.

Amazon Prime had the UK rights so that was a fantastic new experience. I fill in as the sports presenter during the holidays on the Radio 2 Chris Evans' Breakfast Show which is the most bonkers and fun show to work on. At the other end of the scale is the Radio 4 Today programme which gives me a chance to do more serious interviews and discuss topics in depth. I am looking forward to Wolves being back in the Premier League so that I can mention them (when editorially necessary of course) on the BBC1 Ten O'Clock News! I also work for the Premier League's global television channel so we will show lots of Wolves stories this season and I'm looking forward to re-introducing them to our global audience. My newest ventures include presenting for Classic FM. We're doing a Classical Music Sporting Countdown with music like Nessun Dorma and Jerusalem and I even sneaked in a couple of Wolves mentions on that show which I presented with Henry Blofeld. Plus I have presented a couple of shows for the Royal Opera House in Trafalgar Square in

front of 10,000 people who are waiting to watch a live opera performance beamed on to a big screen from the Royal Opera House. I think you can probably tell that I like variety!

Are there any highlights of your career so far?

I love big sports events so absolute highlights have to be the Brazil World Cup – what a brilliantly football-mad country – reporting at the London 2012 Olympics, commentating at the Rio Olympics, and covering my first US Open. My first Champions League final was in my relatively early days of live reporting for BBC London News but it was Arsenal against Barcelona – an amazing first Champions League final to go to! I found myself getting very emotional being part of the BBC Wimbledon team

when Andy Murray won his first title in 2013, and it was also a sporting hero high to present a show with John McEnroe called 6-Love-6, a tennis phone-in show on BBC 5 Live a couple of years ago. An interesting Wolves highlight was reporting on Wolves'

community projects for Match of the Day and one piece involved getting Marcus Hahnemann, Jamie O'Hara and Adam Hammill to Zumba dance at Molineux... they didn't know what was happening to them!

How would you describe media broadcasting as a career and what are the main qualities you feel you need to show?

Gosh that's a difficult question! Broadcasting is changing so quickly at the moment. There are so many different ways to broadcast these days from the conventional television/radio to streaming/youtube/Instalive etc. But the main qualities needed probably stay the same in that I always say you need a passion. If you are passionate about a subject, then it shows in the way you talk about it. I ended up once at a lecture about how you make whisky, not something I know anything about but the person speaking was so passionate about the whole process that I found it utterly fascinating! Passion, patience and perseverance are definitely needed in broadcasting. There is a lot of multiskilling these days too.

If you had any advice for young people setting out in their careers – whatever career it may be – what would that be?

Absorb as much information as you can from the people you admire in whatever industry you are in. Watching and learning from the best in the business is an easy, and free, way to see how successful people get to where they are. Doing things that take you out of your comfort zone is also a good way to push yourself and means you are on a fast learning curve! I'm still often out of my comfort zone!

Finally, back to Wolves, what did you think of last season and what are your hopes for the return to the Premier League?

Last season felt unusual! No angst and pacing around. It was similar to watching England at the World Cup in Russia, it all seemed a bit too calm and composed when I've been used to a lifetime of nail biting tension. But I have also got photos of the league table from various points during the season with Wolves at the top of the table, because I kept thinking we might not stay there. Then we went on to get automatic promotion and become champions, both with games to spare. What a season! Nuno has done a brilliant job with the team and it's testament to him that players are signing extensions to contracts and looking forward to staying with Wolves rather than thinking about moving to other, so called 'big clubs'.

And, how much are you looking forward to reading out details of a Wolves win on the BBC's Saturday night news?

Haha, I can't wait! I might have a slightly bigger grin than normal and an extra twinkle in my eye that evening. It's been a long time coming! Maybe I could wear a gold top...or that might be going a little bit too far...

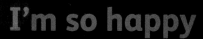

I'm so happy to be here and join the guys, it's an

AMAZING FEELING

to play again for Wolves. **Last season was a good one** and I hope this one will be better.

FORMER LOAN
LOCKED-
DOWN

LEO
BONATINI

Leo Bonatini might have been something of a surprise signing when he arrived on loan from Al-Hilal in Saudi Arabia. But the Brazilian striker made a superb initial impact, with 12 goals in his first 20 league games. Goals were harder to come by in the second half of the season, but Nuno had seen enough of Bonatini's all-round play to decide to make the deal permanent.

CHAMPIONS,
I am very happy
and proud to be back.
I want to help the team
ACHIEVE
OUR OBJECTIVES.

FORMER LOAN
LOCKED-DOWN

RUBEN VINAGRE

Ruben Vinagre spent a year on loan at Wolves from AS Monaco before becoming a fully fledged Wolf!

The exciting left back made 13 appearances in all competitions, and notched an impressive individual goal in the 4-0 win at Burton Albion

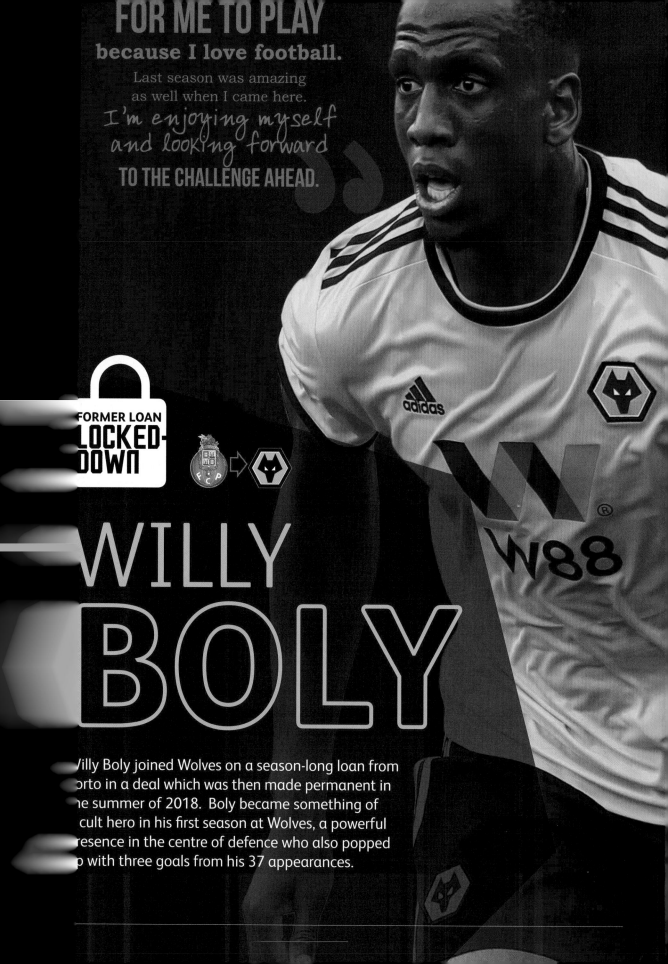

FOR ME TO PLAY

because I love football.
Last season was amazing
as well when I came here.
I'm enjoying myself
and looking forward
TO THE CHALLENGE AHEAD. "

FORMER LOAN
LOCKED-DOWN

WILLY
BOLY

Willy Boly joined Wolves on a season-long loan from Porto in a deal which was then made permanent in the summer of 2018. Boly became something of a cult hero in his first season at Wolves, a powerful presence in the centre of defence who also popped up with three goals from his 37 appearances.

> ## "It's a dream come true,
> *I always watched the Premier League as a kid and I'm looking forward to it*
> ## AND I'LL DO MY BEST."

DIOGO JOTA

Diogo Jota was another player to hugely impress during his loan spell, to the degree that Wolves reached agreement with Atletico Madrid in January to make his stay permanent at the end of the season. He was the club's top scorer in that debut campaign, notching 18 goals from 46 appearances.

Young Wolves' RECORD YEAR!

It was a record year for Wolves memberships during the title-winning 2017/18 season, and Young Wolves had an absolute ball!

Here are a few photos from the fun and games from last season.

From the Christmas Party for the Dribblers and Young Wolves to the Halloween Open Training Session, sellout mascot packages to the End of Season Awards Dinner, the club's young fans once again had the chance to mix with the first team squad and enjoy experiences and memories to last a lifetime.

Now onto more of the same in the Premier League!

Wolves Junior Memberships
Season 2018/19

£12 · Ages 0-3

Wolves Dribblers
membership
Season 2018/19

Wolves Dribblers benefits include:
- Plush baby on board sign for your car
- Signed certificate from head coach
- Exclusive events
- A free copy of the Official Wolves Sticker Album for 2018/19
- **Plus lots more!**

£15 · Ages 4-11

Young Wolves
membership
Season 2018/19

EXCLUSIVE GIFTS

Young Wolves & #WolfPack benefits include:
- Priority booking for home, away and cup tickets
- 100 loyalty points
- Exclusive member events
- Discounts from selected partners
- Opportunity to claim one of 5,000 FREE tickets to be made available to junior members across the Premier League season
- A free copy of the Official Wolves Sticker Album for 2018/19
- **Plus lots more!**

EXCLUSIVE GIFTS

£17.50 · Ages 12-16

#WolfPack
membership
Season 2018/19

EXCLUSIVE GIFTS

wolvesmembership.co.uk | 0371 222 1877

53

FROM THE ARCHIVES:

A decade on

Our 'From the Archives' section in this year's Annual focused on promotion and the Premier League, particularly apt given the team's rise into the Premier League.

First up we look back to a decade ago, and the last team to reach the Premier League, when the class of 2008/09 won the Championship title.

As with last season, Mick McCarthy's team blazed a trail in the division's second tier for most of the campaign and, even during a difficult time at the start of 2009, never relinquished their hold on the top spot.

So let's take a pictorial trip down Memory Lane and remember the team of ten years ago which also took Wolves to the Premier League, focusing particularly on the celebrations at the end!

FROM THE ARCHIVES:

Five Great Premier League wins

★ ★ ★ ★ ★

While the club have of course enjoyed many top flight seasons and famous top flight wins prior to the introduction of the Premier League in 1992, this is only our fifth season in the rebranded top division.

So, before we add to our list of famous Premier League wins, here we have picked out five of our best prior to this season.

25/10/03
WOLVES 4-3 LEICESTER CITY

The comeback of all comebacks as West Midlands hosted East, Wolves up against Foxes. At half time the visitors were in cruise control at 3-0 to the good thanks to goals from Les Ferdinand (2) and Riccardo Scimeca. But Wolves somehow responded. Colin Cameron scored twice, including a penalty, and Alex Rae levelled matters before Henri Camara converted Denis Irwin's cross four minutes from time. Cue pandemonium!

 WOLVES: Oakes, Irwin, Butler, Craddock, Naylor, Gudjonsson (Newton 22), Cameron, Rae, Camara, Blake, Miller (Kachloul 45). Subs: Murray, Iversen, Luzhny.

 LEICESTER: Walker, Curtis, Elliott, Taggart, Rogers, Gillespie (Nalis 65), Izzet, Scimeca, Scowcroft, Ferdinand (Bent 64), Dickov (Hignett 64). Subs: Coyne, Stewart.

17/01/04
WOLVES 1-0 MANCHESTER UNITED

A famous win for Wolves who were struggling in their first ever season in the Premier League. Manchester United were the reigning Premier League champions and expected to roll Wolves over at Molineux, but that didn't happen. They certainly enjoyed more of the possession, but Wolves – complete with United old boys Denis Irwin and Paul Ince – held firm, with Kenny Miller's run and finish on 66 minutes securing a famous three points.

 WOLVES: Oakes, Irwin, Craddock, Butler, Naylor, Newton, Ince, Rae, Kennedy, Miller, Iversen (Ganea 80). SUBS: Cameron, Clyde, Kachloul, Ikeme.

 UNITED: Howard, O'Shea, Ferdinand (Brown 50), Silvestre, Fortune, Fletcher (Bellion 65), Keane, Phil Neville (Forlan 68), Ronaldo, Scholes, Van Nistelrooy. SUBS: Butt, Carroll.

12/12/09
TOTTENHAM HOTSPUR 0-1 WOLVES

A day of milestones, this. Wolves' first win in London since 1976, and first successive wins in the top flight for 26 years. And Spurs, boasting attacking threats including Robbie Keane and Jermain Defoe, had swamped Wigan 9-1 in their previous home game. But Mick McCarthy emerged triumphant from his first managerial battle with Harry Redknapp thanks to an all-round performance packed with grit and determination, and the slightest of touches from Kevin Doyle to a Nenad Milijas free kick with just three minutes on the clock.

SPURS: Gomes, Bassong, Dawson, Corluka, Assou-Ekotto, Lennon, Huddlestone, Palacios (Modric 59), Kranjcar (Dos Santos 78), Keane (Crouch 59), Defoe. SUBS: Alnwick, Hutton, Rose, Bale.

WOLVES: Hahnemann, Stearman (Iwelumo 80), Craddock, Berra, Ward, Henry, Edwards (Foley 60), Milijas (Mancienne 70) Doyle, Ebanks-Blake, Jarvis. SUBS: Hennessey, Castillo, Surman, Maierhofer.

29/12/10
LIVERPOOL 0-1 WOLVES

Another historic win as Wolves prevailed at Anfield for the first time in 27 years, since Steve Mardenborough had upset the applecart in 1984 with his only ever goal in the gold and black. Stephen Ward was the hero this time, returning to his former striker position and earning redemption for a previous red card at Anfield by latching onto Sylvan Ebanks-Blake's pass and sliding the ball past Pepe Reina. Wolves had been bottom prior to kick off, but victory took them above West Ham and, incredibly, only four points adrift of a Liverpool side which was struggling under Roy Hodgson.

LIVERPOOL: Reina, Johnson, Skrtel, Kyrgiakos, Konchesky (Aurelio 73), Meireles (Cole 73), Lucas, Kuyt, Torres, Ngog (Babel 62). SUBS: Jones, Agger, Maxi, Poulsen.

WOLVES: Hennessey, Zubar, Stearman, Berra, Elokobi, Hunt, Foley, Milijas, Jarvis (Edwards 89), Ward (Fletcher 78), Ebanks-Blake. SUBS: Hahnemann, Batth, Jones, Mujangi Bia, Bent.

05/02/11
WOLVES 2-1 MANCHESTER UNITED

Another Molineux win against Manchester United, and this one could never be left off the list. United were unbeaten in their previous 24 league games of the season, and 29 league games in total, while Wolves were again occupying the Premier League's bottom spot. Not to mention that United led through Nani after just three minutes. But George Elokobi headed home on ten minutes, and was also very close to the ball when Kevin Doyle did the same on 40, and Wolves held on for a famous win against the team who would go on to win the title and reach the Champions League final.

WOLVES: Hennessey, Zubar, Stearman, Berra, Elokobi, Hammill (Ward 64), Henry, O'Hara (Foley 59), Milijas (Ebanks-Blake 88), Jarvis, Doyle. SUBS: Hahnemann, Craddock, Edwards, Fletcher.

UNITED: Van Der Sar, Rafael, Vidic, Evans (Smalling 65), Evra, Nani, Carrick (Scholes 46), Fletcher, Giggs, Berbatov (Hernandez 65), Rooney. SUBS: Kuszczak, O'Shea, Anderson, Owen.

PLAYER

Matt
DOHERTY
Born: **16/01/92**
Position: **Defender**

Ivan
CAVALEIRO
Born: **18/10/93**
Position: **Forward**

Ruben
NEVES
Born: **13/03/97**
Position: **Midfielder**

Rui
PATRICIO
Born: **15/02/88**
Position: **Goalkeeper**

Bright
ENOBAKHARE
Born: **08/02/98**
Position: **Forward**

Morgan
GIBBS-WHITE
Born: **27/01/00**
Position: **Midfielder**

Diogo
JOTA
Born: **04/12/96**
Position: **Forward**

Romain
SAISS
Born: **26/03/90**
Position: **Defender/Midfielder**

Joao
MOUTINHO
Born: **08/09/86**
Position: **Midfielder**

Will
NORRIS
Born: **08/06/86**
Position: **Goalkeeper**

Leander
DENDONCKER
Born: **15/04/95**
Position: **Defender/Midfielder**

PROFILES

 **Ryan**
BENNETT
Born: 06/03/90
Position: **Defender**

 **Danny**
BATTH
Born: 21/09/90
Position: **Defender**

 **Raul**
JIMENEZ
Born: 05/05/91
Position: **Forward**

 **Helder**
COSTA
Born: 12/01/94
Position: **Forward**

 **Willy**
BOLY
Born: 03/02/91
Position: **Defender**

 **Conor**
COADY
Born: 25/02/93
Position: **Defender/Midfielder**

 **Jonny**
OTTO
Born: 03/03/94
Position: **Defender**

 **John**
RUDDY
Born: 12/08/93
Position: **Goalkeeper**

 **Ruben**
VINAGRE
Born: 09/04/99
Position: **Defender**

 **Kortney**
HAUSE
Born: 16/07/95
Position: **Defender**

 **Leo**
BONATINI
Born: 28/03/94
Position: **Forward**

 **Adama**
TRAORE
Born: 25/01/96
Position: **Forward**

GOING FOR
OLD GOLD!

'Old Gold New Challenge' – that was the tagline as Wolves revealed their new kit – the first to be produced by Adidas – for the 2018/19 season.

And it was a return to the more traditional old gold colour worn by some illustrious Wolves teams back in history!

The away kit meanwhile was a modern white and black number, with both being very well received by Wolves supporters who were particularly pleased to see the team sporting adidas's iconic three stripes.

Here a few of the lads model the new kit which Wolves are wearing in the Premier League this season.

ON SALE NOW
#OldGoldNewChallenge

THE ANSWERS...

Page 26 - Wolfie's Fun Page

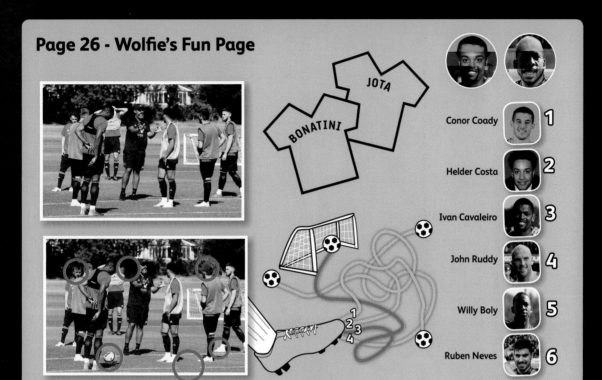

Conor Coady — 1

Helder Costa — 2

Ivan Cavaleiro — 3

John Ruddy — 4

Willy Boly — 5

Ruben Neves — 6

Page 44 - It's a Date!

1. (B) June

2. (C) December

3. (A) March

4. (C) April

5. (C) May

6. (B) October

7. (A) January

8. (B) July

9. (B) November

10. (A) February

11. (B) September

12. (A) August

Page 27 - The Big Wolves Wordsearch

Where's Wolfie?

Wolfie has hidden somewhere in the crowd! Can you find him?